GILES

Giles

The Collection 2027

EXPRESS NEWSPAPERS

CASSELL

First published in Great Britain in 2026 by Cassell,
an imprint of Octopus Publishing Group Ltd
Carmelite House,
50 Victoria Embankment
London EC4Y 0DZ
www.octopusbooks.co.uk

An Hachette UK Company
www.hachette.co.uk

The authorized representative in the EEA is Hachette Ireland,
8 Castlecourt Centre, Dublin 15, D15 XTP3, Ireland (email: info@hbgi.ie)

Cartoons supplied by British Cartoon Archive

ISBN 978-1-78840-676-5

A CIP catalogue record for this book is available from the British Library.

Printed and bound in China.

1 3 5 7 9 10 8 6 4 2

MIX
Paper | Supporting responsible forestry
FSC® C144853

Contents

Introduction by Dr Tim Benson

The initial idea of reprinting Carl Giles's cartoons as an annual began when he was at the now defunct Sunday newspaper, *Reynolds News*, during the Second World War. In November 1940, a reader had written to the editor to say: "I know all about the paper shortage, but what about a Giles annual? God knows we need some sort of Christmas box of this kind in these grim days to send to people." However, the newspaper did not have the readership or the finances to publish it. This changed when Giles joined Express Newspapers in 1943. They had had great success beforehand with his predecessor Sidney Strube, who had had an annual of his *Daily Express* cartoons published every year since 1926. The Giles annual appeared for the first time in 1946 and has been published annually at Christmas ever since.

For Giles, one of the great delights of putting the annual together was creating the front and back cover. These beautifully crafted, full-colour covers, which were always meticulously detailed, were obviously a labour of love. They usually took Giles several months to complete, often involving many revisions and additions. When he submitted the cover for the 1986 annual, showing a stately home with famous statues carefully copied from photographs, Giles warned the production staff that it represented "six months of trial and error and has so many patches stuck on for alterations that it will break if you drop it". In 1963, he would have been furious when the finished artwork for the 1964 cover was turned down because it was considered too downbeat rather than reflecting a festive spirit. Giles, like his most infamous creation, Grandma, could be quite a curmudgeon himself. For the front cover, Giles had drawn the younger members of the Giles Family and their friends dancing to the latest hits of the "Swinging Sixties", much to the consternation of Grandma and Dad. On the back cover, Grandma and Dad had turned the tables on them by turning the record player off whilst Dad sang, I assume off-key, an old song to the accompaniment of Grandma playing the violin. The effect clears the room of all teenagers in the house. An angry Giles had to go off, with little time to spare, and create something not only a little bit more festive, but slightly more cheerful, too.

Not only was the front cover a sizable undertaking, but Giles also found that the selection of material for the annual was something of a headache. His daily cartoons were, of course, topical, in that they related to a news story the previous day. The problem was that when reproduced in the annual months later, many of the cartoons had lost their meaning. They were difficult if not impossible to comprehend without some form of written context. As Giles explains, "one of my most difficult tasks is finding enough self-explanatory cartoons to fill it...working on the same day as the paper is produced, to keep as near to the topical news as I can, the idea gets over on the day. But a year later most of the public have forgotten the scene." One solution was to add explanatory notes, but that meant even more work for him on top of his already heavy workload and charitable commitments. As a consequence, many of the cartoons that could not be easily interpreted were simply dropped.

Giles also excluded cartoons about which he felt he had originally been too harsh. In 1964, for example, the pirate radio station Radio Caroline started broadcasting from a ship moored off the Suffolk coast, and he drew a cartoon of Dad speaking to his radio, calling the disc jockey a "banal, treacly-mouthed patronising creep" (see overleaf). This was certainly his view of many DJs, including the likes of Jimmy Saville, but, on this occasion, he left the cartoon out of the annual, because "it would have appeared to many people as being perhaps a little unkind". Giles also took the opportunity to revise some of the mistakes he had made in his cartoons before they were reused in the annuals. Readers helped in this matter, by often writing in to correct him on any errors. Giles always strove for accuracy when it came to vehicles, mechanical parts, train engines and military uniforms, but he did once draw somebody with two left hands and, on one occasion, three feet! Giles confessed that a lot of these mistakes were made "in the usual rugby scrum to make deadline".

Having written one biography of Carl Giles whilst presently working on another, I was delighted and honoured to be asked to

"And a Happy New Year to *you* — you banal, treacly-mouthed, patronising creep."

Daily Express, 31 December 1964

write this year's introduction to the annual. In my opinion, Giles is, with the exception of Hogarth, the greatest social cartoonist this country has ever produced. It is of no surprise that over the years that followed the Second World War, Giles became a Fleet Street legend. During his heyday, people would buy the *Daily Express* purely to view his cartoon. For 80 years now, the annuals continue to give a rich visual and historical insight into British life. *Sunday Express* journalist Nathaniel Gubbins stated that a Giles annual was "a day-by-day, week-by-week record of English history as it happens. Look at the cartoon and look at the date and you will find you are living recent history over again."

Writing this year's introduction has made me a member of a very illustrious club. For I follow in the footsteps of such luminaries as Margot Fonteyn, Spike Milligan, King Charles III, Sean Connery, Tommy Cooper, Eric Morecambe, Frank Sinatra and Sir John Betjeman, amongst other famous names, who have all contributed introductions to the Giles annual. The majority of them either reminisced about the impact his cartoons had had on their own lives or commented on how well he had humorously captured the absurdities of British life. Sean Connery, however, rather let the side down by having basically nothing really to say about Giles apart from the fact that it had been his turn to introduce the anthology.

The Giles annual regularly reached the Christmas bestseller booklists, proving itself, time and time again, to be the perfect stocking-filler. Even today, 31 years after the cartoonist's death, it is as popular and hilarious as ever. Not surprisingly it remains the longest running annual of cartoons published anywhere in the world.

Dr Tim Benson
The Political Cartoon Gallery

DIY & Gardening

The Buildings Restrictions (War-Time Contraventions) Act 1946, aimed at regulating wartime building work that did not meet building codes and planning rules, became law two days after this cartoon appeared.

"I suppose you've read that you can now be fined up to £5,000 and get seven years for doing unessential building."

Sunday Express, 24 March 1946

A 24-hour stoppage by members of the Electrical Trades Union on 18 and 19 January 1954 was followed by a week-long strike in London later in the month.

"The electricians' strike doesn't really affect us – Father does all his own electrical repairs."

Daily Express, 19 January 1954

The first London Boat Show, held at Olympia, ran from December 1954 to January 1955 and clearly inspired the Giles family.

"I might have known that this family could not go to a boat show and just look at boats."

Daily Express, 4 January 1955

From 1949 to the early 1990s, Scouts and Cubs took part in Bob a Job Week in April each year to raise money.

"WHO had no right to punch his nose just because he walked on my wet cement?"

Sunday Express, 22 April 1962

This frustrated gardener has no sympathy with the aim of National Nature Week – which took place from 18 to 25 May 1963 – to highlight the need to conserve wildlife.

"Of course I know it's National Nature Week and I promise nothing of the sort!"

Daily Express, 23 May 1963

Three weeks earlier, the New Towns Act, which authorised increased financing for the building of new towns to alleviate severe housing shortages, had received Royal Assent.

"Best excuse for getting out of doing the garden I've heard – 'They'll probably be building a city on it in 1970.'"

Sunday Express, 22 March 1964

Supertanker SS *Torrey Canyon* hit rocks off the coast of Cornwall in March 1967, spilling more than 100,000 tonnes of crude oil. Hundreds of miles of coastline as far as Spain and France were severely damaged.

"To think we didn't go to the seaside because of oil on the beaches."

Sunday Express, 26 March 1967

Costly garage bills have driven Father and Grandma to tackle some probably ill-advised DIY repairs on Father's Land Rover.

"I gave them one of Dad's garage bills to play with."

Daily Express, 4 August 1970

The 1971 Census introduced a number of new questions, which the children seem to be enjoying answering with great creativity.

"Well thank you very much, that sure takes care of your Grandma's record – now how about your Father?"

Sunday Express, 18 April 1971

1972 marked a return to British Summer Time after a three-year experiment with British Standard Time, when Britain remained an hour ahead of Greenwich Mean Time all year round.

"Dad, have a look and see if my tortoise is awake now summer time's started."

Sunday Express, 19 March 1972

Canine skin was still used occasionally to make gloves and shoe-linings in the early 1970s – a practice that had been more common in the 1950s because of post-war leather shortages.

"Dad just said the firm who wants to make 'em into gloves and overcoats has got a case."

Sunday Express, 9 April 1972

Legislation including the 1970 Equal Pay Act and the Women's Liberation Movement saw a shift away from sexual discrimination in the 1970s, with Father apparently in wholehearted support.

"There's certainly no discrimination between the sexes in this house. I let the women graduate from menial kitchen duties to concrete mixing and so forth."

Sunday Express, 4 February 1973

Father understandably feels Mother should be concentrating rather than being distracted by the health of Captain Mark Phillips – who had married Princess Anne the previous month – and the on-again, off-again relationship between Elizabeth Taylor and Richard Burton.

"Isn't it wonderful, Mum – Mark's tummy's better and the Burtons are together again."

Daily Express, 11 December 1973

This was at a time of high building costs, but Father's hopes of saving money are about to come tumbling down along with the extension.

"Mum, you know the new extension Dad's building himself to save massive builder's bills?"

Sunday Express, 2 March 1975

One of the coldest ever recorded, Easter 1975 featured widespread snowfall, but Father is not to be deterred from the first lawn cut of the year.

"Nothing's going to stop him giving the lawn its Easter hair cut with his new mower."

Sunday Express, 30 March 1975

Father is having the last laugh on this one as Carol's boyfriend takes over the garden toil.

"Well, he did run on a bit to your dad about the old boys moving over to make jobs for the younger ones."

Sunday Express, 26 September 1976

Father seems rather forbearing in light of the children's re-enactment of the St. George legend straying onto his flower bed and Grandma's brutal hedge trimming.

"St. George to Dragon – I give you ten seconds to get off my new flower bed – over and out."

Sunday Express, 23 April 1978

The 1979 Iranian Revolution triggered an international energy crisis, as oil production dropped dramatically. Fortunately for the state of the lawn, this talented mechanic has found a way around the petrol shortage.

"Slip over the pub and tell your dad bad luck, I've repaired his old hand mower."

Sunday Express, 10 June 1979

Jack is indeed flat out in the summer heat but not working on the shed, as his wife fondly believes.

"This sudden heat doesn't worry my Jack – nothing stops him working."

Daily Express, 21 June 1979

An unwelcome reminder to Father and Ernie of what Mother expects done on the DIY front ahead of any fishing trips. The open coarse fishing season runs from 16 June each year.

"Coarse fishing starts Tuesday – just two days to finish painting the house, finish building the shed..."

Sunday Express, 14 June 1981

Father's plan to economise by buying a goat to eat the grass evidently did not take into consideration goats' reputation of devouring almost everything with enthusiasm.

"Mind the new lawnmower – dad couldn't decide between a ride on air-cushioned or cylinder type."

Sunday Express, 28 March 1982

A “war” between rival lawnmower companies Flymo and Qualcast, featuring aggressive advertising, took place in the early 1980s.

“It’s your dad – he’s invited them to hold their duel on our lawn.”

Daily Express, 14 April 1983

The previous month had been one of the hottest on record, with drought conditions leading to a hosepipe ban. The month ended with heavy rain, thunder and lightning.

"You're still liable for prosecution, sir, the ban has not been officially lifted yet."

Daily Express, 2 August 1983

In 1984, British Summer Time began with a period of particularly wet, windy and gloomy weather.

"Now the clocks have gone forward, Dad will have the nice light evenings to work on the garden."

Sunday Express, 25 March 1984

Traditionally the weekend for DIY, Easter revamps don't always go according to plan as evidenced by this couple and their unintentionally airy bathroom.

"Next – 'Make hole to take two inch waste-pipe.'"

Sunday Express, 7 April 1985

Newspapers had covered the story of a homeless man temporarily taking up residence in a shed in the London garden of Labour MP Tony Benn, while he was away.

"No, we haven't got a tramp moved in at the bottom of the garden, like Tony Benn – that's dad."

Sunday Express, 14 April 1985

Forty years on from Victory in Europe Day and Father's good intentions remain just that...

VE Day 1945: "Now it's over, I'll get some leave and repair that gutter and put a couple of boards in that fence."

VE Day 1985

Sunday Express, 5 May 1985

Ernie and Bridget seem resigned – but understandably not overjoyed – at the prospect of another Christmas with the results of Father's woodworking skills awaiting them under the tree.

"Christmas comes but once a year – another fort for me and another doll's cradle for you."

Sunday Express, 8 December 1985

A catastrophic reactor explosion at the Chernobyl nuclear power plant in Ukraine on 26 April 1986 caused a radioactive cloud to drift over much of Europe and the UK in the following weeks.

"That's the encouragement I like – according to the weatherman the wind has changed again so I'm wasting my time putting them in."

Sunday Express, 11 May 1986

Beating the summer heat with enthusiastic post-work thirst-quenching has led to some equally enthusiastic – if erratic – mowing.

"Why do I think my husband is drunk in charge of a lawnmower? Because he's cutting the wrong lawn for a start!"

Daily Express, 21 August 1986

Negotiations were taking place between the United States and the Soviet Union that led, at the end of 1987, to the INF (Intermediate-Range Nuclear Forces) Treaty limiting the use of short- and intermediate-range nuclear missiles.

"The faster they step up the Peace Talks, the faster he digs."

Daily Express, 31 March 1987

Outspoken Health Minister Edwina Currie had reportedly advised a woman to prioritise paying for dental care over decorating her house.

"I'd gladly give up decorating the living room so Vera could have her new gold tooth."

Sunday Express, 31 January 1988

Housework

Renowned mountaineer Sir John Hunt helped set up and was the first director of the youth development programme, the Duke of Edinburgh's Award.

"Basically youth starts by being idealistic, anxious to prove itself and serve..." – Sir John Hunt, Conference at Harrogate.

Daily Express, 13 October 1960

Following the end of a moratorium on nuclear testing, in 1962 the United States conducted 31 hydrogen bomb tests in the Pacific.

"No one's going to convince YOU that all this is a waste of time now they've resumed H-bomb tests, is he?"

Daily Express, 27 April 1962

In 1964, the government encouraged women to go to work, offering tax relief for childcare, to try to address labour shortages.

"Just let mine come and tell me he's found me a nice little spare-time job in a factory."

Daily Express, 27 August 1964

In the 1960s, there was an assumption that increasing automation would soon eliminate most jobs and that leisure should be emphasised as compensation. A philosophical point somewhat lost on the very busy women in this cartoon.

"Pity you dozed off, dear – you missed the bit about their aim being to provide more leisure to cushion the impact of automation."

Daily Express, 10 September 1964

A strike by bakery workers in 1965 had significant impact on bread supplies, leading to rationing. Luckily for the Giles family, they have Grandma's "light-weight" baking to look forward to as an alternative.

"One of Grandma's light-weight, home-made loaves coming up."

Sunday Express, 21 November 1965

Joseph Grimond had resigned as leader of the Liberal Party two days earlier and was succeeded by Jeremy Thorpe.

"It's not the passing of their Jo Grimond that worries me – it's the passing of routine service in this house"

Daily Express, 19 January 1967

The 18th Miss World beauty pageant took place at the Lyceum Ballroom in London two days after this cartoon appeared, and was won by Australia's Penelope Plummer.

"Would Mr. Universe be good enough to inform Miss World what he would like in his sandwiches?"

Daily Express, 12 November 1968

In 1969, scientists Robert Edwards and Patrick Steptoe, working with nurse and embryologist Jean Purdy, succeeded in fertilising a human egg in a test tube, paving the way for the birth of the first "test-tube" baby in 1978.

"I think you ought to go and see what they're up to. They've been in the shed for hours with Ernie's Magic Chemistry set."

Sunday Express, 16 February 1969

The FA Cup Final between Leeds and Arsenal had taken place the previous day, the former's 1–0 win missed by this football fan who had been allowed his rest.

"Yes, I read it – I let mine put his feet up and he fell asleep all through the Cup Final."

Sunday Express, 7 May 1972

Debates around The Licencing Act (Scotland), which came into force later in the year, were considering a number of possible provisions, including pubs being able to apply for a children's certificate, which would allow those under the age of 14 entry for meals.

"Well, how did baby like his first legal visit to a pub?"

Sunday Express, 29 February 1976

A few weeks earlier, *Consumers' Research Magazine* had rated the reliability, among other features, of various washing machine models.

"My automatic washing-up machine never breaks down – he wouldn't dare!"

Daily Express, 11 February 1977

A strike by one of its key component suppliers forced British Leyland to lay off over 17,000 employees in August 1977. "We want to work" was a familiar slogan at the extensive strikes by Leyland workers throughout that year.

"She saw them on TV chanting 'We want to work.'"

Sunday Express, 28 August 1977

Despite service regulations, high inflation and low pay in the late 1970s forced many military personnel to take on additional civilian work to make ends meet.

"Albert! This is Sergeant Revett – he does light housework to supplement his military pay."

Daily Express, 30 November 1977

President of the National Union of Mineworkers, Joe Gormley had presided over the overtime ban that had forced the government to introduce a three-day working week in 1973. A 1979 newspaper article quoted him as saying everyone should be allowed to work one day a week only.

"I'd like to see Joe Gormley get mine to work one day a week."

Sunday Express, 7 October 1979

Three days earlier, members of the Special Air Services (SAS) had stormed the Iranian Embassy in London to rescue hostages held in a siege.

"Message from HQ: 'All SAS men will enter by the back door.'"

Daily Express, 8 May 1980

The rail network ground to a halt in 1982 as members of train drivers' union ASLEF took industrial action to protest the eight-hour day being replaced with flexible working hours, or rostering.

"Don't rush back from the pub – I'm doing the washing instead of cooking the dinner – flexible rostering."

Sunday Express, 4 July 1982

Mr. Olympia, a professional body-building contest, was taking place at London's Wembley Conference Centre.

"Do you think you could manage to lift his Teddy off the floor for him?"

Daily Express, 7 October 1982

Released in UK cinemas in December 1982, *E.T. The Extra-Terrestrial* was a huge hit – something that Mother, with Christmas baking in full swing, has no time to dwell on.

"Vera – If I've got any tears to shed this morning I give you my written guarantee right now they're not for E.T."

Daily Express, 9 December 1982

Mother's prospect of catching up with all the household chores after the Bank Holiday weekend looks anything but "a nice easy day".

"You're lucky, you can have a nice easy day to get over the holiday."

Daily Express, 30 August 1983

An massive eight-day blockade by French truck drivers in February 1984 caused major disruption and traffic chaos, with lengthy delays throughout the country.

"I'll give him just a couple of days of this: 'Madame Francoise didn't cook it like this in Lyons during the Great Blockade.'"

Sunday Express, 26 February 1984

62 This member of the "weaker sex" is taking full of advantage of the judge's sexism to enjoy a very comfortable Sunday afternoon.

"Golf is out, Vic, thanks to that clever judge and his 'Women are the weaker sex.'"

Sunday Express, 18 August 1985

Influential restaurant critic Egon Ronay wrote and published a series of guides to British restaurants and hotels for 30 years, the first edition in 1957.

"She read Egon Ronay's report that it's fashionable to go out for a Continental breakfast, then she comes back and has a traditional English one as well."

Daily Express, 4 February 1986

 That February was one of the coldest on record in the UK, but the England cricket team were enjoying the Caribbean sunshine, playing a five-match Test series that the West Indies won 5–0.

"My heart bleeds for our poor cricketers losing out there in all that terrible sun."

Sunday Express, 23 February 1986

Prime Minister Margaret Thatcher had launched the "Tidy Britain" campaign earlier in 1988, when she was photographed picking up litter in St. James's Park, and frequently compared the spotless streets of cities in other countries with those in Britain.

"Achtung Herbie, here she comes again."

Daily Express, 1 November 1988

Relaxing

Father, with his feet up, dreams of life on the high seas with his yacht prize. Mother's vision of Father's sailing prowess is rather less generous.

The Dream of a Yacht

Daily Express, 14 July 1955

Britain's programme to develop a hydrogen bomb began in 1954. Extremely unlikely though it is that the giant egg contains carbide and heavy water, it is certainly going disturb Grandma and Vera's peace.

"It's full of carbide and heavy water."

Daily Express, 18 April 1957

A quiet afternoon of reading is broken by this furious football supporter. The previous day, Nottingham Forest had beaten Aston Villa in the FA Cup Semi-Final.

"Well, will your team be in the Final, dear?"

Sunday Express, 15 March 1959

This sport fan is enjoying his summer in the garden watching the first day of the Test Match between England and India at Trent Bridge.

"I didn't know I'd married an athlete until we got television."

Daily Express, 4 June 1959

 In 1959, during the Cold War, France refused to host additional US aircraft so they were instead moved to US air bases in Britain.

"Daddy says what's wrong with sending another 20,000 US planes over here from France – you couldn't make more blasted row than you make already."

Daily Express, 10 July 1959

Government funding to promote tourism to the UK consistently increased during the early 1960s. Father seems to think that is enough excuse for the dishevelled appearance of both the garden and himself as he enjoys the unseasonably warm spell that occurred in mid-March of 1961.

"And WHY can't I sit here looking like this with the Government spending more than any other country in promoting Britain as a tourist attraction?"

Daily Express, 16 March 1961

The BBC began testing colour television in 1955, but didn't launch it until July 1967, starting on BBC2 with coverage of Wimbledon.

"That's what I like – HE can't watch black and white TV since he's seen the coloured TV demonstration."

Daily Express, 11 May 1961

Father has taken drastic measures to stop Ernie's "fool questions" disturbing his fireside Sunday afternoon.

"Because since he read that he's been sitting here asking me a lot of fool questions – that's why."

Sunday Express, 6 October 1963

It had recently been announced that The Beatles were to be appointed Members of the Order of the British Empire, for their contribution to music and the economy. The nomination was very controversial, leading some previous recipients to return their medals.

"I don't recall us kicking up all this dust when Olivier got gonged for playing Hamlet."

Daily Express, 17 June 1965

The day after this cartoon appeared, Prime Minister Harold Wilson announced an election for just over a month later, his Labour Party winning with a sweeping majority.

"It's too bad of Mr. Wilson to keep us all in this state of nervous tension about the election date."

Sunday Express, 27 February 1966

This “accidental” soaking suggests “his highness’s” wife feels he could make better use of a Sunday afternoon than spending it dozing in a deckchair.

“Whoops! Sorry, your Royal Highness.”

Sunday Express, 5 May 1968

Rumours – later proven unfounded – were circulating that newspaper and magazine tycoon Cecil King was plotting with others to overthrow Harold Wilson's Labour government.

"Charles dear, perhaps daddy doesn't want a man-to-man talk on Cecil King and Mr. Wilson."

Sunday Express, 12 May 1968

A television documentary covering a year in the life of the Royal Family had been broadcast the previous day, attracting over 30 million viewers.

"Another marked difference between the Royal Family film and ours is they manage to get the top of their heads in for a start."

Sunday Express, 22 June 1969

The previous day, 41-year-old Pancho Gonzales had beaten 25-year-old Charlie Pasarell in a match that lasted more than five hours – the longest match in Wimbledon history at the time.

"I fear the great daddy of tennis in this family has been neglecting his winter training."

Daily Express, 27 June 1969

A two-week strike by around 4,500 teachers, in support of increased pay, began on 1 December 1969. Over 300 schools were affected but, unfair as it seemed to some pupils, not all schools were closed.

"If there's one thing I can't abide it's a little brother whose teachers are on strike when mine aren't."

Daily Express, 4 December 1969

After weeks of international speculation about where it would come down, Skylab, the United States' first space station, dramatically fell uncontrolled to Earth on 11 July 1979, scattering debris across the southern Indian Ocean and Western Australia.

"Stand by! Skylab returning to earth – over."

Sunday Express, 8 July 1979

The second European Economic Community election to be held in the UK, the 1984 election was won by the Conservatives but with a smaller majority than in 1979.

"Rufus! Farmer says sorry to interrupt your day off he gave you to go to the EEC Elections, but he wants the key to the toolshed."

Daily Express, 14 June 1984

Neighbours

News of the first cuckoo – unofficially heralding the start of spring – and its demise, has distracted Father enough to allow the man next door to get rid of his rubbish in a most unneighbourly way.

"Dad, will you write a letter to the *Express*? Fred's just heard the first cuckoo – and GOT it!"

Daily Express, 22 March 1949

A country-wide strike ordered by the National Union of Railwaymen for midnight on 9 January 1955 had been called off.

"Close shave that time, Florrie – nearly had 'em at home all day."

Sunday Express, 9 January 1955

Ernie and the twins are wisely stealing away before the source of Mother's bunch of daffs becomes known to Father.

"My boy gave the wife a nice bunch of daffs for Mother's Day."

Sunday Express, 12 March 1961

British car manufacturer Jaguar unveiled its iconic E-Type model, initially for export only, to great acclaim in March 1961.

"There goes one of your 'Holier than thou' brigade. Husband's on night shift at Jaguars."

Daily Express, 6 April 1961

The one-day London Underground strike that took place the day after this cartoon was published caused chaos across the capital.

"I could understand you moaning about me bringing work home during the Transport Strike if I was a keeper at London Zoo."

Sunday Express, 4 February 1962

The season of good will does not extend to forgiveness where damage – however unintentional – to precious cars is involved, it appears.

"They don't sound like the words on that nice little Christmas card you sent us."

Daily Express, 28 December 1962

The previous day's papers had warned of winter power cuts. At a time when the virtues of the new electricity supergrid were being extolled, this is particularly unwelcome news.

"Well – let's get the Easter eggs on the boil."

Daily Express, 19 September 1963

NASA's Gemini 9A spacecraft, which had launched at Cape Kennedy (now Cape Canaveral) two days earlier, is probably not going to successfully shift the blame from Ernie for the damage about to be inflicted on Mr. Jones's greenhouse.

"Dad – I think a piece of Gemini 9 is just going to land on Mr. Jones's greenhouse."

Sunday Express, 5 June 1966

A recent newspaper headline had announced that a council house tenant had opened their garden to the public.

"Worst case of keeping up with the Joneses I've seen for a long time."

Daily Express, 22 August 1967

Francisco Franco's dictatorship and Spain's blockade of Gibraltar in 1968 led to the disapproval of many – including all these neighbours – of holidaying in Spain.

"So much for free wheeling down the road after dark so they won't know we're leaving for a Spanish holiday."

Daily Express, 9 May 1968

The 1969 Divorce Reform Bill, which became law a year later, had been the subject of much news coverage. It introduced "no-fault" divorce and safeguards for fair financial provision for both parties.

"It'll be interesting to see what they do when they come to Tibby."

Sunday Express, 26 January 1969

A group of miners' wives from Wakefield in Yorkshire had made headlines by refusing to do any housework until their husbands – on unofficial strike – returned to work.

"FLORRIE, we've got a blackleg at number 132."

Daily Express, 24 October 1969

Toy drums do not good neighbours make, it seems. One wonders who thought a drum would make the ideal gift for the Giles children...

Sunday Express, 27 December 1970

Miners striking over pay were picketing power stations, leading to a shortage of electricity, forcing businesses and shops to close and the introduction of a three-day week to conserve power. A state of emergency was declared the day after this cartoon appeared.

"My Harry won't risk using the lift with possible power cuts."

Daily Express, 8 February 1972

The 1973 Arab–Israeli War led OPEC (Organization of Oil Producing Countries) to impose an embargo on countries, including Britain, that supported Israel. Major fuel shortages resulted, with oil prices quadrupling and long queues at petrol stations.

"I'm not hoarding, it's empty, but I like to give the Gestapo next door something to report."

Daily Express, 20 November 1973

 Both Millwall and Chelsea supporters were infamous for their hooliganism – something that Giles deplored – in the 1970s.

"Poor little devil, I used to worry about him when he went off to war – but going off to see Millwall v Chelsea..."

Sunday Express, 5 September 1976

Larry Hagman's character J. R. Ewing, powerful Texas oil tycoon, famously wore a 10-gallon hat in the popular TV drama, *Dallas*.

"It's a shame her making him wear that – he doesn't even watch Dallas."

Sunday Express, 23 March 1980

In mid-August, French fishermen began blockading major ports, stranding over 20,000 tourists at peak holiday season. These weary travellers' relief at finally being home is about to be marred by news of Tibby's new arrivals.

"I hadn't the heart to tell them their Tibby's had six lovely little kittens."

Daily Express, 21 August 1980

A report commissioned by Scotland Yard and made public the previous day had concluded that London's police force was rife with dishonesty, racial prejudice and drunkenness.

"I think they're fascinated with your new image since they read you're all drunken racist bullies."

Sunday Express, 20 November 1983

In 1984, the case of Sewell vs Cohen saw Snaresbrook Crown Court adjudicate in deciding who was the rightful owner of a cat which was named Marmaduke by John Sewell and Sunny by Monty Cohen.

"I'm not taking you to court over who owns it, but it'll be the Old Bailey for the pair of you if I catch it near my goldfish pond again!"

Sunday Express, 17 June 1984

The trend for competitive vegetable-growing had begun four years earlier, but apparently still cannot supersede newspaper coverage of tennis player Martina Navratilova, cricketer Ian Botham and trade unionist Arthur Scargill.

"I see Navratilova, Botham and Scargill still get more coverage in the Press than prize marrows."

Sunday Express, 1 July 1984

In the 1986, the UK government stepped up its campaigns against drink-driving, encouraging people to report drunk drivers anonymously.

"Never mind about serve me right for hiding up a tree all night to catch him coming home from his pub – call the Fire Brigade!"

Sunday Express, 16 November 1986

In January 1987, Prince Edward, now Duke of Edinburgh, left the Royal Marines four months into a 12-month officer-training course.

"My old man runs on about Prince Edward going soft, but we know who has to go out in the cold to get the milk in this house."

Daily Express, 8 January 1987

Father's electrical skills are sometimes questionable (see the cartoon on page 11), and this time the whole street is suffering the repercussions.

"Stand by for tidings of good cheer from the neighbours – Dad's just blown every fuse in the road."

Sunday Express, 11 December 1988

Organised by charity Keep Britain Tidy, the country's first National Spring Clean Day was launched in 1989.

"Knock off this clean up Britain Mum – they've already labelled us the most anti-social snobs in the avenue."

Daily Express, 9 February 1989

 Soviet leader Mikhail Gorbachev had just ended an historic two-day trip to the UK, visiting Prime Minister Margaret Thatcher in Downing Street and Queen Elizabeth II at Windsor Castle.

"I know they love Gorbachev but I'm not having vodka and balalaika all day."

Sunday Express, 9 April 1989

Pets

Demand for budgies was very high in the 1950s, their small size and easy care needs making them much in demand as the perfect pet.

"I'd show him who's favourite in this house if they ever let him out for a fly round the room."

Sunday Express, 15 September 1957

It looks like every member of the family will be getting a hamster – or two – for Christmas.

"Fellers, you know that hamster we've bought Grandma for Christmas...?"

Daily Express, 13 December 1960

Secretary of State for War, John Profumo, had resigned ten days earlier after admitting he had lied to Parliament about his relationship with the model Christine Keeler. A major political scandal, the so-called Profumo Affair, sparked an outcry at the "moral collapse" of the Conservative Party.

"While the whole nation's on the subject of morals I'm going to have a word about that damn Tom of theirs."

Daily Express, 14 June 1963

Two days earlier a dog named Pickles had become famous for finding the Jules Rimet football World Cup trophy, which had been stolen from an exhibition a week earlier.

"But not you, mate. Empty salmon tins and old boots are about your top score."

Daily Express, 29 March 1966

"This sort of thing isn't going to help my public image, Paddy me boy."

Daily Express, 7 March 1967

 The Crufts dog show had taken place in Olympia, London, the previous day. The Dalmation that won Best in Show for the year presumably knew more about winning ways with the judges than Butch's rough and ready methods.

"You, of course, had to be different. You had to go and pick the Judge up by his ears."

Sunday Express, 11 February 1968

It would seem Mummy's pills aren't doing what they are supposed to...
The oral contraceptive pill was introduced in the UK in 1961.

"That's funny, we've been feeding them on Mummy's pills for ages."

Sunday Express, 14 December 1969

The global flu pandemic – also known as the Hong Kong Flu – that broke out in 1968 killed over a million people in the two years that followed, and the children are taking no chances with their new pet.

"Don't fly off the handle, Grandma – we're only using your bed while our Christmas present's got flu."

Daily Express, 30 December 1969

The day before, a health expert had addressed a meeting of the British Veterinary Association on the dangers of infections carried by pets.

"I think you're as safe kissing Butch as you know who."

Daily Express, 17 September 1970

As part of its campaign against unwanted pregnancies, the Health Education Council had just issued a controversial pamphlet featuring notorious 18th-century courtier, Giacomo Casanova, on the cover.

"Pity you can't train that damn dog of yours to read a few Casanova posters."

Daily Express, 31 December 1970

Unusually poor harvests in many of the world's major food production areas led to a global food crisis in the early 1970s. The cost of food, including animal feed, rose sharply – a fact that looks unlikely to bother the cat.

"In view of the animal feeding stuffs crisis do you think we might persuade you-know-who to supplement his rations by catching the odd mouse?"

Daily Express, 8 August 1972

A general election – resulting in the first hung parliament since 1929 – took place two days after this cartoon appeared.

"Everyone else in the road have had their polling cards, Butch. I repeat – everyone else in the road have had their polling cards, Butch..."

Daily Express, 26 February 1974

A recent global shortage and soaring costs had made beef a rare treat in many British households. Alas, Butch is the only member of the Giles family who is going to enjoy this particular Sunday joint.

"As we haven't had beef for so long I thought I'd be rash and treat ourselves to a piece of sirloin."

Sunday Express, 12 May 1974

Phone charges had increased the previous day, a three-minute local call from approximately 0.5 to 0.7 pence and a national call from 4.5 to 5.4 pence.

"It's all right Dad – Bill's hamster has reversed the charge for his call to Butch."

Daily Express, 2 October 1975

The country was heading towards a severe drought, prompting awareness campaigns on the need to conserve water. The Blennerhassett Report from the committee set up to review legislation relating to drink-driving had been published the previous day.

"Grandma isn't going to like you topping your goldfish up with her gin to save water. Nor is the Government Drink-Drive Committee."

Daily Express, 29 April 1976

In 1976, a series of celebrations and commemorations in the United States led up to the 200th anniversary of the adoption of the Declaration of Independence on 4 July.

"That wasn't very nice, Butch – biting Grandma in America's bicentennial week."

Daily Express, 8 July 1976

The previous day, Giles's team Ipswich – in their first appearance – had won the FA Cup Final, beating Arsenal 1–0.

"We know your team won. Never mind how he got it – take it back!"

Sunday Express, 7 May 1978

In the 1970s, there was increasing public and political concern at the rising rate of crime in the UK and whether the police had the sufficient resources to deal with this.

"The guardian of the house is demanding overtime."

Daily Express, 19 October 1978

The newspaper headline refers to the popular BBC TV programme *All Creatures Great and Small*, featuring Yorkshire vet James Herriot, the first series of which was broadcast from 1978.

"I haven't been drinking, Mrs. Mackinlay, but I'm afraid your wee cat has."

Daily Express, 28 November 1978

The moment the parrot – which was going to have a significant impact on daily life – joined the Giles family.

"You've bought Grandma a WHAT for Christmas?"

Sunday Express, 21 December 1980

This was the night of the 1981 census. Attila the Hun, Grandma's parrot, is making completing the paperwork complicated.

"Hold it, Dad! Attila the Hun's just laid another egg."

Daily Express, 5 April 1981

Butch has seen to it that the Giles family are never going to learn if it is true that geese make better guard dogs.

"Dad, you know the Consumers Association said a goose is a better guard dog than a dog?"

Daily Express, 24 November 1981

Father does not seem to appreciate the parrot's "helpfulness" in volunteering his services to venture out in what was one of the severest winters ever recorded.

"No problem – he'll come out in the Land Rover and tow you home – only eight miles from here, you said?"

Sunday Express, 10 January 1982

The Wildlife and Countryside Act – protecting birds, animals, plants and habitats – became law in October 1981 and was implemented in phases in 1982.

"Meet the latest member of the family – from today bats become a protected species."

Daily Express, 28 September 1982

A Public Accounts Committee Report had found that the administration costs of dog licences were not covered by the revenues they generated, so there was debate in parliament over the merits of increasing the licence from 37½ pence to £10.

"If your licence does go up to £10, in future the slippers will be delivered right here."

Sunday Express, 8 July 1984

Natalie the cat appears to appreciate soft-hearted Vera providing the garden birds with winter sustenance to plump them up nicely.

"Mind you don't make them too fat to fly away from the cat!"

Sunday Express, 20 January 1985

Dorothy Rea had died recently, leaving her fortune of £2.8 million to animal charities. Her brother Ben died just a few days later and bequeathed £7 million to his cat, Blackie.

"You're wasting your time, cat – the most she'll leave you is her lucky charm and half a bottle of peppermints."

Daily Express, 12 May 1988

It seems this picky poodle is in no hurry to get to the annual Crufts dog show, which was won in this particular year by a border collie.

"How the hell do I know what bacteria is in it – we've got one hour to get to Crufts – eat!"

Sunday Express, 12 February 1989

Two days after this cartoon appeared, the Convention on International Trade in Endangered Species approved a worldwide ban on the ivory trade.

"We rescued him from the London Zoo."

Daily Express, 15 October 1989

At the Door

The postman's cavalier approach to delivering mail shows just what he thinks of the directive that the public need not give a Christmas box (money or a small gift) as a token of appreciation.

"Why couldn't they wait till AFTER Christmas before they told them about this no Christmas box business?"

Daily Express, 16 December 1947

Father has evidently had enough of media coverage of electioneering in the run-up to the 1959 general election.

"Psst!"

Daily Express, 10 September 1959

A letter from the tax office is rarely good news, particularly at this time of the year.

"And a Happy New Year to you too!"

Daily Express, 30 December 1960

Long-running TV show *This Is Your Life* featured host Eamonn Andrews surprising a special guest before taking them into a studio to go through their life story with help of appearances from friends and family.

"Would you mind telling the old fool that everyone who calls isn't someone from the BBC trying to shanghai her for 'This is Your Life.'"

Daily Express, 9 February 1961

The delivery of an array of musical instruments to the child next door, coupled with news that the Soviet Union had resumed nuclear testing, is making for a depressing Sunday.

"Minnie – did I hear you say things couldn't get much worse?"

Sunday Express, 3 September 1961

In the early 1960s, Strontium-90, a radioactive isotope from fallout from nuclear weapons testing, was discovered in British milk.
Although anxiety was high, the British government assured the public that milk consumption was safe.

"A plague on you and your fall-out testers."

Daily Express, 26 October 1961

The Big Freeze of winter 1962 to 1963 saw temperatures fall to an average of –2˚C for more than two months. Snow started on Boxing Day and remained for months, while power cuts hit thousands of homes.

"You'll be lucky, mate."

Daily Express, 13 January 1963

A major 1966 Egg Marketing Board campaign saw "Egg Chicks" visiting households at breakfast time. Those who had eggs on the menu were given a Premium Bond, those that didn't were given free eggs. "Chanticleer" is a medieval name for a rooster.

"Morning, Chanticleer."

Sunday Express, 13 March 1966

Earlier in the month, Prime Minister Harold Wilson had announced that the UK would be making a second application to join the Common Market (European Economic Community).

"As I told the lady next door, once we're in the Common Market, WHAM! Up'll go the price of food."

Daily Express, 9 May 1967

The fashion collections for Spring/Summer 1969 took place in Paris in the last of week of January with major fashion houses, including Chanel, holding their shows on 28 and 29 January.

"Here we are – straight Paris Collection – in rave black, with plunging lace neckline and chic off-white cuffs."

Daily Express, 28 January 1969

A newspaper article published a few days earlier had quoted a health official arguing against keeping elderly people alive through long-term medical intervention.

"Put the doctor down, Grandma. He's come about Ernie's measles, not to bump you off."

Daily Express, 2 May 1969

This cartoon appeared in the run-up to the general election which took place on 18 June 1970, the Conservatives defeating Labour and securing a majority of 30 seats.

"'Ullo. Which public spirited party has come to nurse us in the art of wise government this time?"

Daily Express, 9 June 1970

150 The country's switch to decimal currency – Decimal Day – had taken place the previous day. There were some complaints that shops and deliverymen were effectively raising prices by rounding up to the nearest pence.

"Shut up before you start! Thanks to decimal chit-chat I'm not half way through yesterday's round."

Daily Express, 16 February 1971

There was a shift against fox hunting in the 1970s, though this busy woman looks a little taken aback to be asked her opinion on the matter.

"Mother! Gentleman from the Polls wants your opinion on Fox Hunting."

Daily Express, 26 November 1972

A recent newspaper article had calculated how much the average housewife would earn if paid the market rate for her domestic work.

"And while you're at it – put me down for laundrymaid, cook, gardener, decorator, nurse, plumber and car-washer for starters."

Daily Express, 27 October 1975

The cost of bread was the subject of much debate in Parliament at the time and Grandma clearly takes a dim view of the price of her loaf. Though it's a brave – and foolish – person who calls her "old girl".

"If the old girl answers, I bet she'll give us an earful."

Daily Express, 13 January 1977

Milk deliveries began to decline from the 1950s and the rumour of scrapping them entirely in 1978 is certainly working in this baker's favour.

"It's an ill wind, as they say."

Daily Express, 26 April 1978

Having announced their engagement in February, the wedding of Prince Charles and Lady Diana Spencer took place on 29 July 1981.

"Your invitation's come, Mam. Please let 'em know if you wish to go by glass wedding coach or open landau."

Daily Express, 28 May 1981

Chancellor of the Exchequer Geoffrey Howe had controversially announced in Parliament a week earlier that Britain's economic recession was ending.

"Go tell mummy Geoffrey Howe says the recession's over, so you can buy two each."

Daily Express, 4 August 1981

Harty, popular television presenter Russell Harty's celebrity chat show, had recently moved to the prime early-evening slot on BBC1.

"Your elephant-trap to catch Russell Harty is working, Grandma – we've got the milkman, the baker, Mrs. Mainwaring's labrador..."

Daily Express, 20 September 1983

The Post Office had announced record pre-tax profits for this year but major disputes at London sorting offices had created a significant backlog in deliveries – neither fact appreciated by Grandma.

"The dog won't go for you but SHE will – about our £116 million profits and her being later than ever."

Daily Express, 19 July 1984

January 1985 was particularly cold with widespread snow, and this "cheery" postman is doing nothing to improve the misery caused by the weather.

"One package holiday brochure for sunny Spain...no stamp, 34p to pay."

Daily Express, 10 January 1985

Cartoons
British Cartoon Archive

All the cartoons in this book were copied from material in Carl Giles's own private archive, a huge collection of artwork, ephemera and correspondence, which is held by the British Cartoon Archive at the University of Kent. Carl Giles had been cartoonist for Lord Beaverbrook's *Daily* and *Sunday Express* for almost 20 years, when on 20 March 1962 the Conservative M.P. Sir Martin Lindsay tabled a motion deploring "the conduct of Lord Beaverbrook in authorising over the last few years in the newspapers controlled by him more than 70 adverse comments on members of the royal family who have no means of replying."

Lindsay was wrong about the royal family having no means of reply. That day Prince Philip also vented his anger at Beaverbrook's campaign, during a press reception at the British Embassy in Rio de Janeiro. According to the paper's Brazil representative, the Prince declared that, "The *Daily Express* is a bloody awful newspaper. It is full of lies, scandal and imagination. It is a vicious paper."

When the *Daily Express* reported this the next day, Giles decided to treat it as a joke. He knew the royal family enjoyed his cartoons; they often asked for the artwork. This had begun in 1948, when Prince Philip was sent a cartoon on the State Opening of Parliament, and over the next few years Giles received a steady stream of requests from Buckingham Palace for original drawings.

Left: *Lord Beaverbrook is marched to the Tower, 22 March 1962.*

Giles drew the diminutive Lord Beaverbrook being escorted through the Traitor's Gate at the Tower of London, with a headsman's axe and block standing ready in the background. The caption repeated Prince Philip's condemnation of the *Daily Express*, but added laconically: "'Ah well,' said Lord B., as they trotted him off to the Tower, 'at least he takes it or he wouldn't know it was a bloody awful newspaper.'"

This was a brilliant response, which did much to defuse the situation. When Giles's cartoon was printed the next day, *Daily Express* staff were surprised to receive a phone call from Queen Elizabeth II's press secretary, with a message for Giles that "Her Majesty requests today's cartoon to commemorate one of her husband's most glorious indiscretions."

Giles sent off the artwork and in May 1962 found himself invited to "a small informal luncheon party" at Buckingham Palace with Queen Elizabeth II and Prince Philip, Duke of Edinburgh. "I was filled with absolute dread," Giles recalled afterwards. "But as soon as she started to talk I was put at my ease… There were about half a dozen corgis running about in a completely uncontrolled state. Suddenly the Queen shouted, 'HEP.' It was like a bark from a sergeant major. The corgis immediately stood to attention. Then filed out of the room."

After the lunch Giles mischievously drew a cartoon of the guests leaving with corgi-savaged trousers. He sent it to the Queen, who returned her thanks through one of her private secretaries, noting that she was "glad that you got away without having lost, at least to the best of her knowledge, so much as a shred of your trousers."

After that Giles became what one *Daily Express* journalist called "a kind of cartooning jester to the royal family." By the time he retired in 1991, the royal family had more than 40 of his original drawings, the largest number being owned by Prince Philip, who shared Giles's anarchic view of the world.

The British Cartoon Archive, based at the University of Kent's Templeman Library in Canterbury, is dedicated to the history of British cartooning over the last 200 years. It holds the artwork for more than 150,000 British political and social-comment cartoons, plus large collections of comic strips, newspaper cuttings, books and magazines. Its website at www.cartoons.ac.uk has over 200,000 cartoon images, including the majority of Carl Giles's published work.